December

Week 52

○ **27. MONDAY**

○ **28. TUESDAY**

○ **29. WEDNESDAY**

○ **30. THURSDAY**

○ **31. FRIDAY**

○ **1. SATURDAY / 2. SUNDAY**

PRIORITIES

TO DO

January

○ 3. MONDAY

PRIORITIES

○ 4. TUESDAY

○ 5. WEDNESDAY

TO DO

○ 6. THURSDAY

○ 7. FRIDAY

○ 8. SATURDAY / 9. SUNDAY

January

○ 10. MONDAY

PRIORITIES

○ 11. TUESDAY

○ 12. WEDNESDAY

TO DO

○ 13. THURSDAY

○ 14. FRIDAY

○ 15. SATURDAY / 16. SUNDAY

January

○ 17. MONDAY

PRIORITIES

○ 18. TUESDAY

○ 19. WEDNESDAY

TO DO

○ 20. THURSDAY

○ 21. FRIDAY

○ 22. SATURDAY / 23. SUNDAY

January

Week 4   01/24/22 - 01/30/22

○ 24. MONDAY

PRIORITIES

○ 25. TUESDAY

○ 26. WEDNESDAY

TO DO

○ 27. THURSDAY

○ 28. FRIDAY

○ 29. SATURDAY / 30. SUNDAY

January

01/31/22 - 02/06/22

○ 31. MONDAY

PRIORITIES

○ 1. TUESDAY

○ 2. WEDNESDAY

TO DO

○ 3. THURSDAY

○ 4. FRIDAY

○ 5. SATURDAY / 6. SUNDAY

February

02/07/22 – 02/13/22

○ 7. MONDAY

PRIORITIES

○ 8. TUESDAY

○ 9. WEDNESDAY

TO DO

○ 10. THURSDAY

○ 11. FRIDAY

○ 12. SATURDAY / 13. SUNDAY

February

Week 7

02/14/22 – 02/20/22

○ 14. MONDAY

○ 15. TUESDAY

○ 16. WEDNESDAY

○ 17. THURSDAY

○ 18. FRIDAY

○ 19. SATURDAY / 20. SUNDAY

PRIORITIES

TO DO

February

○ 21. MONDAY

PRIORITIES

○ 22. TUESDAY

○ 23. WEDNESDAY

TO DO

○ 24. THURSDAY

○ 25. FRIDAY

○ 26. SATURDAY / 27. SUNDAY

February

○ 28. MONDAY

PRIORITIES

○ 1. TUESDAY

○ 2. WEDNESDAY

TO DO

○ 3. THURSDAY

○ 4. FRIDAY

○ 5. SATURDAY / 6. SUNDAY

March

○ 7. MONDAY

PRIORITIES

○ 8. TUESDAY

○ 9. WEDNESDAY

TO DO

○ 10. THURSDAY

○ 11. FRIDAY

○ 12. SATURDAY / 13. SUNDAY

March

○ 14. MONDAY

PRIORITIES

_____

_____

○ 15. TUESDAY

_____

_____

_____

_____

_____

○ 16. WEDNESDAY

TO DO

_____

_____

○ 17. THURSDAY

_____

_____

_____

○ 18. FRIDAY

_____

_____

_____

_____

○ 19. SATURDAY / 20. SUNDAY

_____

_____

_____

March

○ 21. MONDAY

PRIORITIES

○ 22. TUESDAY

○ 23. WEDNESDAY

TO DO

○ 24. THURSDAY

○ 25. FRIDAY

○ 26. SATURDAY / 27. SUNDAY

March

Week 13   03/28/22 – 04/03/22

◯ **28. MONDAY**

PRIORITIES

◯ **29. TUESDAY**

◯ **30. WEDNESDAY**

TO DO

◯ **31. THURSDAY**

◯ **1. FRIDAY**

◯ **2. SATURDAY / 3. SUNDAY**

April

○ 4. MONDAY

PRIORITIES

○ 5. TUESDAY

○ 6. WEDNESDAY

TO DO

○ 7. THURSDAY

○ 8. FRIDAY

○ 9. SATURDAY / 10. SUNDAY

April

Week 15

○ 11. MONDAY

PRIORITIES

○ 12. TUESDAY

○ 13. WEDNESDAY

TO DO

○ 14. THURSDAY

○ 15. FRIDAY

○ 16. SATURDAY / 17. SUNDAY

April

Week 16

○ 18. MONDAY

PRIORITIES

○ 19. TUESDAY

○ 20. WEDNESDAY

TO DO

○ 21. THURSDAY

○ 22. FRIDAY

○ 23. SATURDAY / 24. SUNDAY

April

○ **25. MONDAY**

PRIORITIES

○ **26. TUESDAY**

○ **27. WEDNESDAY**

TO DO

○ **28. THURSDAY**

○ **29. FRIDAY**

○ **30. SATURDAY / 1. SUNDAY**

May

○ 2. MONDAY

PRIORITIES

○ 3. TUESDAY

○ 4. WEDNESDAY

TO DO

○ 5. THURSDAY

○ 6. FRIDAY

○ 7. SATURDAY / 8. SUNDAY

May

Week 19

○ 9. MONDAY

PRIORITIES

○ 10. TUESDAY

○ 11. WEDNESDAY

TO DO

○ 12. THURSDAY

○ 13. FRIDAY

○ 14. SATURDAY / 15. SUNDAY

May

○ 16. MONDAY

PRIORITIES

○ 17. TUESDAY

○ 18. WEDNESDAY

TO DO

○ 19. THURSDAY

○ 20. FRIDAY

○ 21. SATURDAY / 22. SUNDAY

May

○ 23. MONDAY

PRIORITIES

○ 24. TUESDAY

○ 25. WEDNESDAY

TO DO

○ 26. THURSDAY

○ 27. FRIDAY

○ 28. SATURDAY / 29. SUNDAY

May

○ 30. MONDAY

PRIORITIES

○ 31. TUESDAY

○ 1. WEDNESDAY

TO DO

○ 2. THURSDAY

○ 3. FRIDAY

○ 4. SATURDAY / 5. SUNDAY

June

○ 6. MONDAY

PRIORITIES

○ 7. TUESDAY

○ 8. WEDNESDAY

TO DO

○ 9. THURSDAY

○ 10. FRIDAY

○ 11. SATURDAY / 12. SUNDAY

June

○ 13. MONDAY

PRIORITIES

○ 14. TUESDAY

○ 15. WEDNESDAY

TO DO

○ 16. THURSDAY

○ 17. FRIDAY

○ 18. SATURDAY / 19. SUNDAY

June

06/20/22 – 06/26/22

○ 20. MONDAY

PRIORITIES

○ 21. TUESDAY

○ 22. WEDNESDAY

TO DO

○ 23. THURSDAY

○ 24. FRIDAY

○ 25. SATURDAY / 26. SUNDAY

June

06/27/22 – 07/03/22

○ 27. MONDAY

PRIORITIES

○ 28. TUESDAY

○ 29. WEDNESDAY

TO DO

○ 30. THURSDAY

○ 1. FRIDAY

○ 2. SATURDAY / 3. SUNDAY

July

Week 27

07/04/22 – 07/10/22

○ 4. MONDAY

PRIORITIES

○ 5. TUESDAY

○ 6. WEDNESDAY

TO DO

○ 7. THURSDAY

○ 8. FRIDAY

○ 9. SATURDAY / 10. SUNDAY

July

Week 28

○ **11. MONDAY**

PRIORITIES

○ **12. TUESDAY**

○ **13. WEDNESDAY**

TO DO

○ **14. THURSDAY**

○ **15. FRIDAY**

○ **16. SATURDAY / 17. SUNDAY**

July

07/18/22 – 07/24/22

○ 18. MONDAY

PRIORITIES

○ 19. TUESDAY

○ 20. WEDNESDAY

TO DO

○ 21. THURSDAY

○ 22. FRIDAY

○ 23. SATURDAY / 24. SUNDAY

July

Week 30

07/25/22 - 07/31/22

○ **25. MONDAY**

PRIORITIES

○ **26. TUESDAY**

○ **27. WEDNESDAY**

TO DO

○ **28. THURSDAY**

○ **29. FRIDAY**

○ **30. SATURDAY / 31. SUNDAY**

August

Week 31   08/01/22 - 08/07/22

○ **1. MONDAY**

PRIORITIES

○ **2. TUESDAY**

○ **3. WEDNESDAY**

TO DO

○ **4. THURSDAY**

○ **5. FRIDAY**

○ **6. SATURDAY / 7. SUNDAY**

August

08/08/22 – 08/14/22

○ 8. MONDAY

PRIORITIES

○ 9. TUESDAY

○ 10. WEDNESDAY

TO DO

○ 11. THURSDAY

○ 12. FRIDAY

○ 13. SATURDAY / 14. SUNDAY

August

○ **15. MONDAY**

PRIORITIES

○ **16. TUESDAY**

○ **17. WEDNESDAY**

TO DO

○ **18. THURSDAY**

○ **19. FRIDAY**

○ **20. SATURDAY / 21. SUNDAY**

August

08/22/22 – 08/28/22

○ 22. MONDAY

PRIORITIES

○ 23. TUESDAY

○ 24. WEDNESDAY

TO DO

○ 25. THURSDAY

○ 26. FRIDAY

○ 27. SATURDAY / 28. SUNDAY

August

○ **29. MONDAY**

PRIORITIES

○ **30. TUESDAY**

○ **31. WEDNESDAY**

TO DO

○ **1. THURSDAY**

○ **2. FRIDAY**

○ **3. SATURDAY / 4. SUNDAY**

September

○ 5. MONDAY

PRIORITIES

○ 6. TUESDAY

○ 7. WEDNESDAY

TO DO

○ 8. THURSDAY

○ 9. FRIDAY

○ 10. SATURDAY / 11. SUNDAY

September

09/12/22 – 09/18/22

○ 12. MONDAY

PRIORITIES

○ 13. TUESDAY

○ 14. WEDNESDAY

TO DO

○ 15. THURSDAY

○ 16. FRIDAY

○ 17. SATURDAY / 18. SUNDAY

September

Week 38

○ 19. MONDAY

○ 20. TUESDAY

○ 21. WEDNESDAY

○ 22. THURSDAY

○ 23. FRIDAY

○ 24. SATURDAY / 25. SUNDAY

PRIORITIES

TO DO

September

09/26/22 – 10/02/22

○ 26. MONDAY

PRIORITIES

○ 27. TUESDAY

○ 28. WEDNESDAY

TO DO

○ 29. THURSDAY

○ 30. FRIDAY

○ 1. SATURDAY / 2. SUNDAY

October

○ 3. MONDAY

PRIORITIES

○ 4. TUESDAY

○ 5. WEDNESDAY

TO DO

○ 6. THURSDAY

○ 7. FRIDAY

○ 8. SATURDAY / 9. SUNDAY

October

Week 41   10/10/22 - 10/16/22

○ 10. MONDAY

PRIORITIES

○ 11. TUESDAY

○ 12. WEDNESDAY

TO DO

○ 13. THURSDAY

○ 14. FRIDAY

○ 15. SATURDAY / 16. SUNDAY

October

Week 42   10/17/22 – 10/23/22

○ 17. MONDAY

PRIORITIES

○ 18. TUESDAY

○ 19. WEDNESDAY

TO DO

○ 20. THURSDAY

○ 21. FRIDAY

○ 22. SATURDAY / 23. SUNDAY

October

Week 43   10/24/22 – 10/30/22

○ 24. MONDAY

PRIORITIES

_____

_____

_____

○ 25. TUESDAY

_____

_____

_____

○ 26. WEDNESDAY

TO DO

_____

_____

_____

○ 27. THURSDAY

_____

_____

_____

○ 28. FRIDAY

_____

_____

_____

_____

○ 29. SATURDAY / 30. SUNDAY

_____

_____

_____

October

○ 31. MONDAY

PRIORITIES

○ 1. TUESDAY

○ 2. WEDNESDAY

TO DO

○ 3. THURSDAY

○ 4. FRIDAY

○ 5. SATURDAY / 6. SUNDAY

November

11/07/22 - 11/13/22

○ 7. MONDAY

PRIORITIES

○ 8. TUESDAY

○ 9. WEDNESDAY

TO DO

○ 10. THURSDAY

○ 11. FRIDAY

○ 12. SATURDAY / 13. SUNDAY

November

11/14/22 – 11/20/22

○ 14. MONDAY

PRIORITIES

○ 15. TUESDAY

○ 16. WEDNESDAY

TO DO

○ 17. THURSDAY

○ 18. FRIDAY

○ 19. SATURDAY / 20. SUNDAY

November

○ 21. MONDAY

PRIORITIES

○ 22. TUESDAY

○ 23. WEDNESDAY

TO DO

○ 24. THURSDAY

○ 25. FRIDAY

○ 26. SATURDAY / 27. SUNDAY

November

○ **28. MONDAY**

PRIORITIES

○ **29. TUESDAY**

○ **30. WEDNESDAY**

TO DO

○ **1. THURSDAY**

○ **2. FRIDAY**

○ **3. SATURDAY / 4. SUNDAY**

December

Week 49   12/05/22 – 12/11/22

○ 5. MONDAY

PRIORITIES

○ 6. TUESDAY

○ 7. WEDNESDAY

TO DO

○ 8. THURSDAY

○ 9. FRIDAY

○ 10. SATURDAY / 11. SUNDAY

December

○ 12. MONDAY

PRIORITIES

○ 13. TUESDAY

○ 14. WEDNESDAY

TO DO

○ 15. THURSDAY

○ 16. FRIDAY

○ 17. SATURDAY / 18. SUNDAY

December

                                             12/19/22 – 12/25/22

○ 19. MONDAY

PRIORITIES

○ 20. TUESDAY

○ 21. WEDNESDAY

TO DO

○ 22. THURSDAY

○ 23. FRIDAY

○ 24. SATURDAY / 25. SUNDAY

December

○ 26. MONDAY

PRIORITIES

○ 27. TUESDAY

○ 28. WEDNESDAY

TO DO

○ 29. THURSDAY

○ 30. FRIDAY

○ 31. SATURDAY / 1. SUNDAY

Made in the USA
Monee, IL
27 September 2021